Armageddon

By Marilyn Hickey

Marilyn Hickey Ministries

P.O. Box 17340 • Denver, Colorado 80217

Armageddon

All scriptures are quoted from the
King James Version of the Bible
unless otherwise indicated.

CONTENTS

Chapter One
Crossroads to War

And when these things begin to come to pass, then look up, and lift up your heads; for your redemption draweth nigh (Luke 21:28).

End-time prophecies are being fulfilled every day. Newspapers tell us about wars and rumors of wars, strife, plagues, famines, pestilence, and earthquakes. Reports show that Christians all over the world are hated, tortured, killed, taken to court, and betrayed by family members. Every night, newscasts tell us about false prophets who are leading many astray and people's love waxing cold. Crime and lawlessness abounds, parents are killing their children, and children are killing their parents.

Our world has gone mad! Every day the devil gains new ground, claiming the hearts and minds of individuals, families, and nations. Yet, I am not afraid. Instead, I am encouraged because Jesus said 2,000 years ago that these things would come to pass in the last days. Each war, famine, plague, and murder shows me that God's plan and purpose for this world are being fulfilled exactly as prophesied.

Mankind's Final Curtain Call?

The entire subject of the end times is shrouded with mystery and heated by centuries of theological debate. No aspect of the end-times, however, is as misunderstood as Armageddon.

While it strikes fear in the hearts of some; to others, the word *Armageddon* has become nothing more than a term signifying the struggle between good and evil or a bloody battle. Used to describe the destruction of the world and the end of mankind, Armageddon is described as a war without winners.

Armageddon *is* a terrible battle that will create a river of blood! It is the final rebellion of Satan and man against God. The Antichrist will gather a global army in Israel and ravage the land on the way to Jerusalem, pillaging cities and killing thousands.

Not once, however, will Satan and his servants lift a sword against the Lord. When Christ returns with His bride to earth, Satan's army is destroyed with the voice of our Savior (Joel 2:11). Therefore, there is no real *struggle* between good and evil because Christ will overcome without lifting a finger.

There *are* winners at Armageddon! God's righteous—Christians and all the Jews who believe Jesus is their Messiah—will receive the title deed to the earth. They will live without evil in their midst. They will be part of the divine process of restoring this world into the paradise it was before man's fall from grace.

Armageddon will not mark the end of mankind. Instead, in bodies that will not die and with hearts that won't break, mankind will begin an eternity of praise and fellowship with our Father, our Savior, the Holy Spirit, and our brethren in Christ.

A Story of Restoration

The entire end-time story is one of restoration. Through the events of the Tribulation and Armageddon, God gives the world back to its original owner—mankind—and returns it to its original state. Through the rapture of the Church and the return of Jesus Christ, people receive glorified bodies that never again experience sin, pain, hunger, sadness, nor death.

The events of the end times bring the story of man's sinfulness full circle. From the beginning, when Adam and Eve sinned, God set up a plan to protect His fallen children, to bring them back to His holy embrace.

Redemption means to "set free" by paying a price. While we were sinners, we were bound by the penalty of sin, which was death. We were controlled by the power of evil. Jesus set us free from this bondage when He paid the price for our freedom. Through His sacrifice, we were restored to our original master, God, and were again

7

allowed into His blessed arms for a relationship with Him.

Adam and Eve didn't understand the magnitude of God's redeeming power. When they sinned, they tried to hide their offense by making their own covering. They thought they could do what only God could accomplish. Covering for sin, or atonement, cannot be established by human hands, so God took an innocent animal and shed its blood in order to make coats of skin to cover the evidence of their sin from His eyes.

God showed Adam what it meant to die because of sin and set a precedent for all men who came after him—redemption from sin can only come from God and can only be done through the shed blood of an innocent victim. We can only be set free from the penalty of death when we accept Christ's covering for our sins.

When man sinned, he (1) lost his soul: *". . . for in the day that thou eatest thereof thou shalt surely die"* (Genesis 2:17); (2) lost his body: *". . . for dust thou art, and unto dust shalt thou return"* (Genesis 3:19); and (3) lost the earth when it passed into the control of Satan.

All Will Be Restored!

Praise God that from the very foundation of the earth He had a plan to save us!

He restored our soul—*"Christ hath redeemed us from the curse of the law, . . . "* (Galatians 3:13). When we accepted what Christ did for us on the Cross, our souls were redeemed.

He will give us perfected bodies—*". . . we ourselves groan within ourselves, waiting for the adoption, to wit, the redemption of our body"* (Romans 8:23). Only after the Rapture, when we receive our glorified bodies, will we realize this redemptive action.

He will retrieve the earth from Satan—*". . . ye were sealed with that holy Spirit of promise, Which is the earnest of our inheritance until the redemption of the purchased possession, . . . "* (Ephesians 1:13,14). This restoration of the earth is a two-fold process that involves both redemption and regeneration. Christ will give the title deed of the earth back to mankind, but God will also bring the earth back to its original condition.

The earth was initially man's property (Genesis 1:26-30), but when man sinned, Satan was able to "purchase" the earth. He possesses the earth now, but I believe God's Word shows that the law of inheritance is greater than that of possession, as indicated by the Jews' return to their nation of Israel. The earth may be Satan's now, but we are the rightful heirs and will hold the title deed to the earth once again.

The difference between an inherited possession

and a purchased possession is the type of ownership. An inheritance was permanent, a purchased property is temporary, much like a rental or lease situation.

Leviticus 25:23-28 says an heir to a property may buy back his land at any time if he has the money and can prove he is an heir or a relative of the heir. Repurchasing land is a legal transaction in which the kinsman or redeemer who is able and willing to pay the price of redemption will, after having paid the price, take the sealed title deed from the man who bought the land and break the seals open. Once opened, the deed is the kinsman's right to evict the purchaser and take possession of the land.

Christ is our Kinsman-Redeemer. He paid the price to possess the earth, but before He can reclaim the land, He must break open the seals to the title deed of the earth.

Christ receives this title deed in Revelation 5 and opens the seals in chapters 6-11. Once all the seals are opened, Christ has the right to evict Satan from the earth, and He does this at the Battle of Armageddon.

A New Earth

The regeneration of the earth is a different process and is set in motion when Christ breaks the seals on the title deed of the earth. With each seal that is broken, the violent forces rock the earth with devastating power.

Regeneration means to "restore something to its original state." It applies to our soul: *"Not by works of righteousness which we have done, but according to his mercy he saved us, by the washing of regeneration, and renewing of the Holy Ghost"* (Titus 3:5); and to the earth: *"And Jesus said unto them, Verily I say unto you, That ye which have followed me, in the regeneration when the Son of man shall sit in the throne of his glory, ye also shall sit upon twelve thrones, judging the twelve tribes of Israel"* (Matthew 19:28).

During the Tribulation, God cleanses the earth with fire. The intense heat causes the glaciers to melt and the oceans and seas to evaporate. A canopy of water forms around the earth, and the great weight of water that is lifted from the earth causes the planet to go back to its original axis. All of this changes the climate to one that is temperate and warm, and an atmosphere that protects us from the sun and space's harmful radiation.

The shifting of the land during all the Tribulation's many earthquakes reconfigure the continents. This world will be barely recognizable. In fact, God calls it a "new world." It will be the

11

same planet we currently live on, but it will be the perfect paradise Adam and Eve knew.

Armageddon

The word, *Armageddon,* appears only once in the Bible: *"For they are the spirits of devils, working miracles, which go forth unto the kings of the earth and the whole world, to gather them to the battle of that great day of God Almighty. And he gathered them together unto a place called in the Hebrew tongue **Armageddon"*** (Revelation 16:14,16). However, this valley is called by other names throughout the Bible, including the Valley of Megiddo and the Valley of Jezreel.

Armageddon means the "hill of Megiddo" in Hebrew. I've visited Megiddo 14 times and I always find this area awesome as I look down from the ruins of King Solomon's once-magnificent horse stables into the Valley of Jezreel, which is what the Israelis call the area today.

The Valley of Jezreel is a fertile, lush valley where grapes, cabbages, barley, and potatoes grow in abundance. The nation of Israel is fed with these crops. It is a calm place, where the morning sunshine chases away the mists of the Kishon River Valley.

Before the Israelis turned this area into the nation's breadbasket in the 1950s, it was primarily a swamp. The area is so flat that the Kishon River runs slowly through the valley. When rains came in the spring, the valley used to flood and leave the land in standing water for several months; but with new flood-control systems, the land is kept clear for farming. It took a great deal of time and hard work to turn this swampland into farmland.

It's hard to believe that this serene setting has been the site of countless battles in history and will be the gathering place for Satan's monstrous army at the end of the Tribulation.

Armageddon In History

In Hebrew, the word *Megiddo* means "assembly, rendezvous." It is derived from *gadad*, which means to "crowd, assemble selves by troops." Its name is well suited.

This valley, which is 55 miles northwest of Jerusalem, was the crossroads of two ancient trade routes: one leading from the Mediterranean Sea on the west to the Jordan River valley on the east, the other leading from Syria, Phoenicia, and Galilee in the north to the hill country of Judah and the land of Egypt on the south.

This triangular plain is 300 square miles and is bordered on the southwest by the Carmel Mountain range, and on the north by the hills of Nazareth. It contains rich farmland because of the soil washed down into it from the mountains of Galilee and the highlands of Samaria. It is also the only east-west valley which divides the mountain ranges of Western Palestine.

The valley lies at the entrance to a pass across the Carmel Mountain range on the main highway between Asia and Africa. It is the key position between the Euphrates and Nile rivers. It was a strategic military site and the scene of many ancient battles, many of which were fought by the people of Israel.

The king of Megiddo was one of 31 Canaanite kings whom Joshua and the Israelites conquered in order to claim the Promised Land (Joshua 12:21). The land then became the possession of the tribe of Manasseh, but the people were afraid to drive out the Canaanites who lived there because they had chariots of iron (Joshua 17:12-18).

Ahaziah, king of Judah, was attacked on the way to Gur when he fled Jehu and then died in Megiddo (II Kings 9:27); and all the people associated with King Ahab's reign, including Jezebel, were assassinated by the followers of Jehu in the Valley of Jezreel (II Kings 9,10). The Philistines were victorious over King Saul there (I Samuel 31:1-3); and the Egyptians mortally wounded Josiah, king of Judah, when he attempted to intercept the army of Pharaoh-nechoh in the valley (II Kings 23:29).

During the judges period, the forces of Deborah and Barak wiped out the army of Sisera in the swampy riverbanks of the Kishon River (Judges 4); and the kings of Canaan who fought against Israel for repossession of the land were defeated in Taanach on the river's edge (Judges 5:19).

The world's final battle, the Battle of Armageddon, begins in this valley, but it will not be fought there. Megiddo is only the gathering place. Once assembled there, the Antichrist's demon-powered army marches in absolute precision down the Valley of Jezreel to the Jordan River valley and head south. They turn west near Jericho and head to Jerusalem, where the Final Battle takes place. This is the Valley of Jehoshaphat.

The End Times

As you study Armageddon and the events leading up to it, it's important to understand that you will not be able to completely see into the future. You won't know exactly when the Rapture will occur, nor can anyone definitely say who is the Antichrist.

God told us that humans only *"... know in part, and we prophesy in part"* (I Corinthians 13:9) because prophecy is a mirror in which we can only see dimly (I Corinthians 13:12). Although the prophecies seem difficult, when you compare scripture with scripture you can see the details unfolding and the full scope of the prophecy taking shape. And each day, as we come closer to Christ's return, new events are revealed that help us understand the things He has shown us in prophecies, dreams, and visions (I Corinthians 13:10).

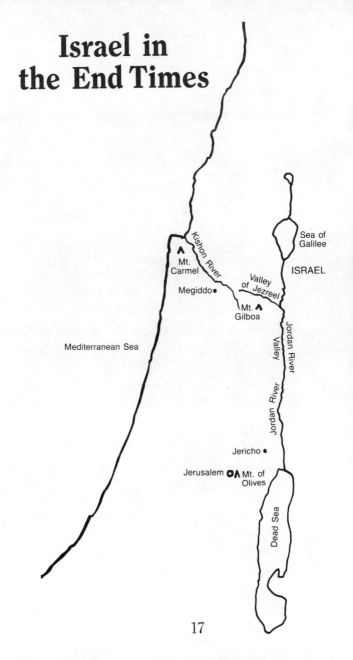

Israel in the End Times

Sea of Galilee

ISRAEL

Mt. Carmel

Kishon River

Valley of Jezreel

Megiddo •

Mt. Gilboa

Jordan River Valley

Mediterranean Sea

Jordan River

Jericho •

Jerusalem ○∧ Mt. of Olives

Dead Sea

Chapter Two
Prelude to a Battle

The reason the Battle of Armageddon is so devastating is that God's patience comes to the point where He can no longer tolerate man's sins. Even in the midst of the outpouring of His wrath, however, God still shows incredible grace and mercy on people who turn from their sins and receive Christ as their Redeemer (Matthew 24:13).

The Rapture

We see many instances in the Bible where God has protected His people from harm. Christ's work on the Cross was the ultimate example of this protection—Jesus paid the price for our sins so we might not die in our iniquity. His blood was shed so ours would not have to flow.

During the Tribulation, God restores this world to its original, pre-curse condition using fire, earthquakes, and floods. These "birthing pains" cause great torment to the people on earth. Many die, others wish they were dead.

God does not want His children to experience these horrors. In a tender act of protection, much like a father pulling his child from the dangers of deep water, Jesus gathers us in His arms.

This gathering together to Christ is the Rapture. Jesus does not return to earth to retrieve us; instead the Christians who are both living and dead meet Him in the clouds: *"Then we which are alive and remain shall be caught up together with them in the clouds, to meet the Lord in the air: . . . "* (I Thessalonians 4:17).

The phrase, *caught up,* in this verse is translated from the Greek word, *harpazo,* which means "pluck, pull, take by force." This same idea of a physical rescue is expressed by Daniel when he prophesied, *". . . and there shall be a time of trouble, such as never was since there was a nation even to that same time: and at that time thy people shall be **delivered**, every one that shall be found written in the book"* (Daniel 12:1). Here, the word, *delivered,* is the Hebrew word, *malat,* which means to "release or rescue speedily."

The word, Rapture, does not appear in the Bible. In modern English, the word means, "a state of ecstasy." While this English meaning can refer to our being in an eternal state of ecstasy when we are finally with our Lord, the term is actually derived from the Latin word, *rapere,* which means "to seize." Thus, our being "seized" into heaven became known as the Rapture.

The world neither sees nor hears Christ at the Rapture—they don't even know anything has happened. The Word says only Christians can hear the trumpet of God and the shout of Jesus as this first seal of the title deed of the earth is opened (I Thessalonians 4:16; Revelation 4:1; 6:1,2). All the world knows is that one second we will be on earth standing side-by-side with our co-workers and friends, and the next second we are gone.

The Rapture happens incredibly fast—*"In a moment, in the twinkling of an eye, . . ."* (I Corinthians 15:52). In this verse, the Greek word for moment is *atomos*, which means "indivisible, an uncut part of time." When something is indivisible, it is so microscopically small that it can't become any smaller. Imagine a measure of time that is so fast that it couldn't be any faster— much like the speed of light. The Rapture of the Church is even faster.

The world can't see what happens to us, but they do come up with many reasons for our departure, including a mass conspiracy or UFOs. Only a few on earth comprehends what has happened and turns to God as a result.

During the Rapture, the dead in Christ rise first (Psalms 17:15; John 5:25; I Corinthians 15:23,52) and then the living are physically caught up into the clouds to meet our Lord for the first time (Revelation 12:5). We then begin our eternal fellowship and worship of Christ (I Thessalonians 4:16,17).

21

Who Will Go?

Anyone who does not believe in God or that Christ is their Lord and Savior will not go in the Rapture. It's important to understand that not every person who calls himself a Christian will be involved in this pre-Tribulation Rapture.

In Revelation 12, the Rapture is pictured as a woman travailing in childbirth. The baby boy she delivers has the authority to *". . . rule all nations with a rod of iron: . . . ,"* and is seen being *". . . caught up into God, and to his throne"* (Revelation 12:5).

We know that the woman is the entire Christian Church because she is clothed with the sun and wearing a crown of 12 stars. The sun shows that she is the light of the world, the 12 stars are the 12 apostles, and the moon under her feet shows that she has the powers of darkness under her (Luke 10:19). The child she delivers is the overcoming Church.

Similarly, in Revelation 3, Christ calls the churches by name. The Laodicean church is left behind at the Rapture. God "spews" this church out of His mouth (Revelation 3:16) because these people do not know Christ. They are the backsliders and lukewarm Christians who warm the pews, waiting for services to get over so they can show off their new cars, clothes, or jewelry. They neither love nor hate Christ—they are indifferent. When they gather for services, they do not invite Him into their midst—He has to stand at the door of their "building" and knock (Revelation 3:20).

The overcoming Christians are the Philadelphia type of church. They are the Christians who keep God's Word and stand on it in patience and faith. Christ promised them that He would keep them *"... from the hour of temptation* (Tribulation), *which shall come upon all the world ... "* (Revelation 3:10). He delivers them from the wrath of the Tribulation.

Satan tries to keep the Church from entering into heaven, engaging in a battle with the archangel, Michael. The dragon won't be able to keep the saints from gathering with Christ, and his bitter contest ends with his expulsion from heaven and the end of his reign as prince of the power of the air (Ezekiel 28:18; Daniel 8:10-13; Revelation 12:7-10).

In anger, Satan sets out to destroy the remnant Church—the lukewarm Christians who turn to God after the Rapture (Revelation 12:12-17). These new Christians flee to the mountains, and nature protects them (Revelation 12:14-16).

The Tribulation

The Tribulation begins after the Rapture. The prophet Daniel called this time period the final week in his vision of 70 weeks in Daniel 9:24-27.

Daniel said that 70 "weeks," or years, would elapse between the Israelites' return to Jerusalem to rebuild the city and Temple and the advent of the Messiah to rule this world. This time period is called the Jewish Age and lasts for 490 years (70 times 7).

Jesus arrived 483 years after the Temple was rebuilt. When the Jews rejected Him, the Jewish Age was suspended and the Church Age began. The Jewish Age resumes again when the Church is raptured, but only one week remains on the clock. This means the time between the Rapture of the Church and the advent of the Messiah as Prince of this world is only seven years.

Daniel described this final week in Daniel 9:27 as a time when the sacrifices and feasts cease and the Antichrist puts his idol, the "abomination of desolation" in the Temple.

At the end of the Tribulation, which is the end of the Jewish age, the Lord comes back from heaven with his saints and angels to "... *make an end of sins, and to make reconciliation for iniquity, and to bring in everlasting righteousness, and to seal up the vision and prophecy, and to anoint the most Holy"* (Daniel 9:24).

This "reconciliation for iniquity" is what Jesus was referring to when He said, *"As therefore the tares are gathered and burned in the fire; so shall it be in the end of this world"* (Matthew 13:40).

The word, *world,* in this verse does not mean "world" in English. It is the Greek word, *aion,* which means "age," as in a period of time. So, at the end of the Jewish Age comes the judgment of the sinners (tares).

The Antichrist

Before the Rapture, the prayers of the saints keep evil from completely running rampant on this earth. Christians are the salt that prevents the decay of Satan's corruption (Matthew 5:13). When our prayers and authority are taken from the earth, the devil's power can finally blossom to its full force and take shape in the person of the Antichrist.

The powers of the devil are hindered, not by the Holy Spirit, but by the Body of Christ. Jesus told us that whatsoever WE bind will be bound in heaven. WE have the authority, and the Holy Spirit does our bidding (Matthew 18:18). So it is the Church, not the Holy Spirit, who hinders the Antichrist from being revealed, and we continue to do so until the moment we are raptured.

I believe the Antichrist is alive today. I don't know his name, but the Word indicates that he is a Jew born somewhere within the borders of the old Assyrian empire (Isaiah 10:5). He is from Syria. In Ezekiel 38:3, the Antichrist is called "Gog"; Ezekiel describes him as the chief prince of Meshech and Tubal. Meshech and Tubal aren't countries, they were grandsons of Noah who settled near the Black and Caspian seas, which are currently bounded by Syria, Turkey, Romania, the Ukraine, Iran, Iraq, and others.

The Antichrist is the head of the northern army, which is referred to in Joel 2:20; and he is called the King of Babylon in Isaiah 14:4 and the Assyrian in Isaiah 10:5. Therefore, the Antichrist comes from a country that is near the Black and Caspian seas, was part of the former Babylonian and Assyrian empires, and is north of Israel. These indicators point to Syria.

The Antichrist could very well have some form of power in a Middle Eastern or European country today, but he currently does not hold a prominent position. He does not come to power until immediately after the Rapture (Ezekiel 28:12-19; II Thessalonians 2:2-4,7-9; Revelation 12:9; 13:3,4; 17:8), when he comes quietly out of obscurity and quickly gains control (Revelation 13:1). His ascent is fueled by war, which is pictured as the second seal, the red horseman (Revelation 6:3).

The Antichrist is a man empowered by Satan. Among his many names in the Bible is the beast, the man of sin, and the son of perdition (II Thessalonians 2:3; I John 4:3).

The Antichrist's personality is fundamentally opposed to Christ's. He exalts himself and says great things, but he doesn't speak the truth. He is very experienced in commerce and making money (Psalms 52:7).

The Antichrist is Judas Iscariot returning to earth in an action that counterfeits Jesus' return to earth. I believe he is Judas because there is a double prophecy in Psalms 55 that shows both Judas' betrayal of Jesus and the Antichrist's betrayal of Israel, revealing them to be the same man.

Also, Judas was more than a man. Jesus called him a devil (John 6:70). The word Jesus used to describe Judas was *diabolos*, which means "accuser, a slanderer" and is one of the names of Satan. Judas was the devil incarnate, just as the Lord Jesus was God incarnate. Also, in John 17:12, Jesus calls Judas the "son of perdition," which is the same name Paul calls the Antichrist in II Thessalonians 2:3.

The Antichrist comes from hell and is superhuman. In Revelation 11:7 he is seen coming out of the bottomless pit, which is the abode of lost spirits and wicked dead, the place of their incarceration and torment (Luke 8:31; Revelation 20:1-3). The Antichrist comes from the bottomless pit because Judas Iscariot was sent there when he died.

In fact, his history as Judas Iscariot is revealed in Revelation 17:8, which shows that he was once on earth and then, in John's day, he was not on earth because he was dead. He will ascend out of the bottomless pit at the time of his rebirth and end up in perdition when Jesus casts him in the Lake of Fire at Armageddon.

The Antichrist is the beast pictured with seven heads and 10 horns. The seven heads are the seven world empires that had conquered and will yet dominate the Israelites—Egypt, Assyria, Babylon, Medo-Persia, Greece, Rome, and the Antichrist. The 10 horns symbolize the 10 nations lying within the borders of these ancient empires that will fall under the Antichrist's rule.

The Antichrist first conquers three countries, which scares seven others to join his confederacy (Daniel 7:24; Revelation 17:12,13,17). After he builds his empire, armies, and reputation, the Antichrist focuses his attention on Israel. He offers his help to make peace with Israel's surrounding nations, and Israel eagerly enters into a seven-year covenant with him (Daniel 9:26,27; 11:22).

He then allows the Jews to rebuild the Temple. This and the peace he brings between Israel and the Arab nations (including the radical Moslem groups united under the Palestine Liberation Organization [P.L.O.]) seems to be such miracles to the Jews that they believe he is their messiah (John 5:43). As a result, Israel's connection with God and their spiritual heritage dries up (Joel 1:10-12).

The world accepts the Antichrist because he is

a genius in seven areas: intellect (Ezekiel 28:3; Daniel 8:23); oration (Daniel 7:20; Revelation 13:2); politics (Daniel 11:21; Revelation 17:17); commerce (Ezekiel 28:4,5; Daniel 8:25; 11:38,43); military and government (Isaiah 14:16,17; Daniel 8:24; Revelation 13:4,7); and religion (II Thessalonians 2:4).

His prowess as a government leader is shown when he welds together opposing forces and unites conflicting countries. He creates an empire out of the former Roman, Greek, Medo-Persian, and Babylonian empires, which currently cover Europe, the Middle East, northern Africa, and parts of Asia.

The Antichrist's tight grip on political, economic, and military systems bring the world under satanic control. Even though he affects the entire world, the Antichrist won't be able to conquer it all—only Jesus will rule the entire world. The extent of his complete authority is limited to the area of the old Roman Empire around the Mediterranean Sea.

While the Antichrist has the world's attention and the Jews' hearts, Satan tries to prove the Antichrist is the messiah. In an imitation of Christ, the Antichrist is killed and, because the people refuse to bury him (Isaiah 14:19,20), the world sees him arise from the dead (Revelation 13:3).

Satan gives his Antichrist new powers to do lying signs and wonders (II Thessalonians 2:9;

Revelation 13:2-7), causing people to revere and worship him (Revelation 13:4). They believe he is God and follow his lead as he persecutes the remnant church (Revelation 13:7,8).

This satanic religion is described as a whore sitting on many waters (Revelation 17:1). I believe the Antichrist's religious system will rule over many people. The kings of the earth fornicate with this whore, and the nations of the earth are drunk with her wine (Revelation 17:2).

The Unholy Trinity

Satan likes to mimic the works of God. God has a Son, so Satan has a son. God has a system of worship, so Satan has a system of worship. God manifests Himself in the form of a Trinity, and so does Satan. In the timing of the Antichrist's resurrection, Satan introduces a new character, the third member of his unholy trinity, the False Prophet.

This second beast arrives on the scene with the power to do lying signs and wonders. He causes people to worship the Antichrist and makes a talking idol of the beast, which he places in the temple (Daniel 9:27; Matthew 24:15; Revelation 13:11-15).

Once this idol—which is called the "abomination of desolation" by Daniel and Jesus—is placed in the Temple, the Jews realize the Antichrist is not from God, but from the devil. They refuse to worship the idol and reject the Antichrist.

The False Prophet orders the death of anyone who doesn't worship the Antichrist (Revelation 13:15). Because Israel had lost her spiritual protection when she made her alliance with the devil, she is powerless to stop the False Prophet and Antichrist's assault.

Israel's economy and agriculture fail (Joel 1:8-10), and the Antichrist strips the country of all its other valuables. The prophet Joel gave a picture of this destruction, saying it will be like the palmerworm, locust, cankerworm, and caterpillar invasions of ancient days, when each new bug eats a part of the crops until even the seeds are gone (Joel 1:4).

The Antichrist's domination of the world tightens as the False Prophet brands people with the mark, name, or number (666) of the beast. No one is allowed to buy or sell unless they do it within the Antichrist's system (Revelation 13:17,18), which is pictured in Revelation 6:5 as the black horseman who is released by the opening of the third seal.

Many systems are currently in place that would allow such control of world trade. Computers, cable systems, microchips, and transportation are advancing quickly. Computer chips have been invented which, when inserted under the skin, can carry a person's vital information, such as name, address, credit history, banking information, employment, and so forth.

Our governments are also relying more and more on a one-world trade system. All of Europe and the three countries of North America are working jointly to bolster their economies. I believe all of this allows the Antichrist to take over easily and manage a world-wide economy.

A world ravaged by war is devastated by this new control over the food markets. A famine begins that destroys animals and kills men (Joel 1:11-18; Jeremiah 14:1-6;), but God orders angels to protect the oil and wine (Revelation 6:6). I believe God is not only calling for the protection of olive oil and grape wine, I believe He is also commanding the angels to protect Jews and Christians.

Throughout scripture, the olive tree symbolizes the Jew's spiritual heritage, so when God orders oil to be protected, He is also calling for the protection of the Jews. The word *wine* in Revelation 6:6 is the Greek word, *oinos,* which is a derivative of the word, *melos,* which means "a part of the body." Christians are called the Body of Christ (Ephesians 3:6).

Nearly every family in the world experiences the ravages of the famine. Things become so desperate that parents eat their children, such as when the

Israelites were being starved during the Babylonian captivity (Lamentations 4:9,10). This death marches across the world and is pictured as a pale horse with death riding him and hell following behind (Revelation 6:7,8; 13:1,11).

Angelic Sermons

Mankind is so preoccupied with its pain that what little energy people have is conserved for the mere act of surviving. The gospel message is preached, however, in a unique move of God—the preaching comes from an angel who declares the gospel from heaven to people on earth. This angel prophesies the fall of the Antichrist's kingdom and religion, telling people not to take the mark of the beast (Revelation 14:6-13).

Some people have said that the Holy Spirit will be removed from the earth at the Rapture. That just doesn't follow what the Word says, because it is through the Holy Spirit's drawing that we come to know Christ (John 16:7-11). People could not be saved during the Tribulation without the Holy Spirit's drawing power.

In fact, the Holy Spirit will move in incredible ways because the greatest time of evangelism on this earth is during the Tribulation. Masses of people turn to the Lord. The masses are going to be so great they they are going to populate the earth during the beginning of the Millennium.

The Bible doesn't give a number of how many

people are saved during this early part of the Tribulation, but Revelation 7:9 says the amount of people saved is more than a man could count. The same scripture says that these Tribulation saints are of "... *all nations, and kindreds, and people, and tongues,* ... " (Revelation 7:9).

Mid-Tribulation Rapture

When Christ opens the fifth seal of the title deed to the earth, we see those Tribulation saints raptured into heaven, standing before the Lamb, dressed in garments washed white as snow and holding palm leaves (Revelation 6:9-11; 7:9,14; 14:12-13).

These palm leaves the saints carry in Revelation 7:9 are very important because they represent victory. In the Bible, the Israelites used palm leaves to remind them of the victories God gave them over their enemies, in each battle, and through every storm. These Tribulation saints standing before Jesus wave their palms to honor the victory God gave them over death and hell.

Catastrophes

The final event before the end of the first 3½ years of the Tribulation is the opening of the sixth seal. Up to this point, heaven had orchestrated the Antichrist's rise to power and the positioning of mankind to make a decision for God or for Satan. With the sixth seal comes the beginning of God's powerful forces moving in a violent way on the earth.

This sixth seal brings great natural catastrophes—the earth quakes, the sun becomes black, the moon turns red, the stars fall, the wind ravages trees and fields, and mountains and islands are moved out of place. People hide in caves and ask the rocks to kill them so they would be saved from God's wrath (Matthew 24:29-31, 38,39; Luke 21:25,26; Revelation 6:12-17).

The entire Tribulation is seven years long and is broken down into two time periods of 3½ years. As the devastation of the sixth seal indicates, the second half of the Tribulation is much worse. In fact, God calls it the Great Tribulation, meaning the horrors are only going to increase for man and the devil.

Chapter Three
Marching on to War

Just before the seventh seal is opened, everything falls silent in heaven for a half hour (Revelation 8:1) while God prepares and delivers His people before the devastating judgments of the final seal are unleashed on the earth. The whole earth stands in awe.

This last 3½ years of the Tribulation, called the Great Tribulation, are filled with much pain, death, and destruction for people and animals, the earth and the heavens. Before this begins, however, God does some very loving things for His people.

First, the angel holding the seal of the living God tells the four angels—who are in charge of the north, south, east, and west winds and will carry out the judgments on the earth—to stop their destructions until God can seal 144,000 people (Revelation 7:3,4).

These 144,000 people are Jews, 12,000 from each of the 12 tribes of Israel. God writes His name on their foreheads (Revelation 14:1) with a mark that I believe is as real and visible as the mark of the beast in Revelation 13:16,17.

The second thing God does is to resurrect the

dead in Christ and to rapture the living Tribulation saints in what is called the Great Harvest Rapture. It is at this time that God separates the wheat from the tares as described by Jesus in Matthew 13:38-43. This rapture is an act of mercy on the gentiles who accepted Christ during this time of great torture, despair, and trouble (Revelation 7:9-17).

The 144,000

What is the difference between these two groups? Why would God leave one group of His people on earth while He takes the other group into heaven? I believe He does this because His full attention is being turned to the Jews at this time and He sends people to them with the message of the gospel. These 144,000 are protected from the coming plagues and the wrath of the Antichrist so they can witness to the world and to Israel.

The 144,000 are the firstfruits of the Jews, people who are spiritual "virgins" (see Revelation 14:4), having never dabbled in a religion that was not from God nor worshiped or followed the beast.

The Bible uses adultery and fornication many times as a picture for spiritual unfaithfulness. These people are called virgins because they stayed true to God and waited for Him to fulfill their desires in life.

"Virgin" can also be taken literally to mean that

these people had not been defiled by sexual indiscretions. The reason this may be taken literally is because Jesus said, "... *as the days of Noe were, so shall also the coming of the Son of man be*" (Matthew 24:37). He explained that people will eat and drink, marry and give in marriage; basically, fulfilling their every desire without respect for self, others, or God—just like people did before the flood.

This carnality is rampant during the Tribulation. Sex and every form of physical indulgence have free reign. However, God always has a remnant. These 144,000 people are set apart by God because (1) they are Jewish, (2) they have remained true to God, (3) they have accepted Christ, and (4) they are physically pure.

Eventually, we see them on Mt. Sion singing "a new song" before Jesus and with the other saints in heaven. Their song can't be learned by other humans on earth (Revelation 14:1-5). Harps play in heaven and all in heaven join in this service of incredible worship. The 144,000 have a special relationship with the Lamb because they recognize that He is their Messiah, Savior, and Redeemer.

The Tribulation Saints

The Tribulation saints are part of the worship service of the 144,000, but this event takes place after they have already held a private service in heaven following their rapture. They stand before the Lord dressed in robes that have been washed white by the blood of the Lamb, playing harps and singing a very important song, the Song of Moses.

This isn't the "new song" of the 144,000; in fact it is a very ancient song. Moses wrote it after God parted the Red Sea, allowing the Israelites to pass into safety, and killed the Pharaoh and his army. Notice how Moses' song of victory tells the story of the Tribulation saints:

. . . I will sing unto the LORD, for he hath triumphed gloriously: . . . The LORD is my strength and song, and he is become my salvation: he is my God, . . . and I will exalt him. The LORD is a man of war: the LORD is his name. Thy right hand, O LORD, is become glorious in power: thy right hand, O LORD, hath dashed in pieces the enemy. And in the greatness of thine excellency thou hast overthrown them that rose up against thee: thou sentest forth thy wrath, which consumed them as stubble. The enemy said, I will pursue, I will overtake, I will divide the spoil; my lust shall be satisfied upon them; I will draw my sword, my hand shall destroy them. Who is like unto thee, O LORD, . . . glorious in holiness, fearful in praises, doing wonders? Thou in thy mercy hast led forth the people which thou hast redeemed: thou hast guided them in thy

strength unto thy holy habitation. Thou shalt bring them in, and plant them in the mountain of thine inheritance, in the place, O LORD, which thou hast made for thee to dwell in, in the Sanctuary, O Lord, which thy hands have established. The LORD shall reign for ever and ever (Exodus 15:1-3,6,7,9,11,13,17,18).

The Israelites still had many trials and battles to face before they could enter and claim the Promised Land, but their song praised Him for what He was going to do as He fulfilled all His promises in their lives. In the same way, the Tribulation saints rejoice in heaven because of their victory over the Antichrist through God's unusual deliverance. They give Him praise for His future and complete work of giving His people their full inheritance.

The entire story of the Exodus and how God delivered the Israelites out of bondage and into a land of promise is a beautiful picture of the end times. The Pharaoh is a shadow of the Antichrist, and the plagues show us a glimpse of what the trumpet/vial judgments are like.

We also see in Exodus that God used nature to speak to man, to show him where he was deceived, and to judge him. God used the plagues to show the Egyptians that their gods were false and powerless. Because they worshipped the Nile, frogs, locusts, and their firstborn children, God used those things to hurt the Egyptians.

The people who paid attention to the plagues and what God was telling them were delivered out of Egypt. Those who placed the mark of God on their doors were spared death in their families during the final plague. Although it was mainly God's chosen, the Israelites, who understood the lessons of the plagues and followed God's commandments, a few Egyptians understood and left during the Exodus.

The same happens during the Tribulation. The people who understand the message of the seven trumpet/vial judgments realize the devil's power counts for nothing when compared with God. Each plague that falls on man and the earth proves that Satan ultimately has no control over the world and is unworthy of their worship.

People who have listened to the messages from heaven and to the many signs that have come from the previous six seals are delivered from the earth in the mid-Tribulation Rapture.

The Two Witnesses

Soon after God "catches away" the Tribulation saints and seals the 144,000, God does another thing to show His great love for people—He brings two men into Israel to preach His Word. These men are called the two witnesses.

I believe the two witnesses are Moses and Elijah because they were on the Mount of Transfiguration with Jesus and their miracles were identical to the ones the two witnesses perform—they cause fire to rain down, turn water into blood, and bring other plagues.

Their purpose in the Tribulation is to harass the Antichrist and call the Jews to worship Jesus. They remain in Israel for 1,260 days, or almost 3½ years (Revelation 11:3).

Zechariah prophesied of these two men in his vision of a gold candlestick and two olive trees (Zechariah 4:2,3). He saw the two witnesses as olive trees. The olive tree is a symbol of the Jews' spiritual heritage. *". . . These are the two anointed ones, that stand by the Lord of the whole earth"* (Zechariah 4:14).

They pour their anointing into the candlestick, which is the symbol for the Church in Revelation. As they preach the Word during the Tribulation, their anointing brings more and more people into Christ's Church (Zechariah 4:12).

The Seven Trumpet/Vial Judgments

Once God's people are protected, the seventh seal on the title deed of the earth is opened. Out of this seal comes seven judgments—four on the earth and three upon mankind.

When we see these seven judgments from heaven, we see them as trumpets blown by angels.

But from earth's perspective, the trumpets look like vials. Compare chapters 6-11 with chapters 12-16 and you will see that they are telling the same story, the first version is seen from heaven, and the second from earth.

For instance, when the second trumpet sounds and a *". . . great mountain burning with fire was cast into the sea: and the third part of the sea became blood; And the third part of the creatures which were in the sea, and had life, died; and the third part of the ships were destroyed"* (Revelation 8:8,9); we likewise see that the second vial affects the sea, making it *". . . as the blood of a dead man: and every living soul died in the sea"* (Revelation 16:3).

The trumpet judgment shows that only a third of the sea dies, but the vial judgment shows that all in the sea dies. Why would the same event have two different outcomes? The difference is because the event is seen from two different perspectives. From heaven's vantage point, we can see the whole earth and that not everything is affected. But when we stand on earth, our view is limited and it appears that the whole earth is affected.

The seven trumpet/vial judgments are discussed several times in the Bible. In Acts 2:19,20 God says, *"And I will shew wonders in heaven above, and signs in the earth beneath; blood, and fire, and vapour of smoke: The sun shall be turned into darkness, and the moon into blood, before that great and notable day of the Lord come."* In Haggai 2:6,7 He said, *". . . Yet once, it is a little while, and I will shake the heavens, and the earth, and the sea, and the dry land; And I will shake all nations, ..."* These words echo Christ's prophecy of the Great Tribulation in Matthew 24:29.

When Jesus opens the seventh seal, these much-prophesied wonders begin with the sounding of the trumpets in heaven.

With the first trumpet/vial, hail mixed with fire and blood falls on earth (Revelation 8:7) in the same way fire and brimstone fell on Sodom and Gomorrah in Genesis 19:24. This fire causes sores to come upon men who have taken the mark of the beast (Revelation 16:2).

The second trumpet/vial affects the water of the seas (Revelation 8:8,9; 16:3), turning it to blood much like when the Nile was judged in Exodus 7:20.

The third trumpet/vial also affects the water, but this time the fire falls on fresh water, poisoning the drinking water with wormwood (Revelation 8:10,11). Revelation 16:4-7 reveals that this contamination has turned the water into blood. This is similar to the punishment God promised the followers of Baal in Jeremiah 9:15, when He said, *". . . I will feed them, . . . with wormwood, and give them water of gall to drink."*

With the fourth trumpet/vial, a third part of the

sun, moon, and stars are darkened; the change in the sun's light increases its heat and scorches men with an intense burning (Revelation 8:12; 16:8,9). God similarly judged the sun in Egypt when he caused darkness to fall over the land. The darkness was so profound that it could even be felt (Exodus 10:21,22).

These first four trumpet/vials have brought great judgments upon the earth, water, and sky. We see a world on fire, thirsty, and scorched. Even though man is terribly tortured by these events, these judgments were meant mainly for nature in order to cleanse the earth of the curse; the next three trumpet/vials are directed toward men exclusively. The pain and torment is so great with these plagues that an angel in heaven cries out, *" . . . Woe, woe, woe, to the inhabiters of the earth . . . "* (Revelation 8:13).

When the fifth trumpet sounds, an angel from heaven who has been given the enormous responsibility of keeping the key to the bottomless pit, opens the pit and looses "locusts" upon the earth. These locusts are demons who have the power to torment men like scorpions. They have bodies like horses, heads like men, hair like women, crowns of gold, teeth like lions, breastplates of iron, wings that sound like chariots running to battle, and tails with scorpion stings. They can't hurt vegetation or the 144,000 Jews;

and they aren't allowed to kill men, only torture them to the point where they beg to die (Revelation 9:1-11).

For five months, people are covered with the sores produced by these demon locusts, living in the darkness that is caused by the smoke of hell covering the sun and moon. People blaspheme God because of their pain, but they do not repent (Revelation 9:2; 16:10,11).

As the plagues plunge the world into chaos, the Antichrist's followers begin to doubt him. The Jews turned against him at the end of the first 3½ years of his reign, and the nations of the world begin to question him. His marvelous miracles can't quench the fires, his tricks can't cleanse the waters, and his charm can't take the pain away.

His grip on the world is loosening. Two of his confederate nations turn against him—the king of the south, probably Egypt, pushes at him and the king of the north, probably Turkey, comes against him (Daniel 11:40). The Antichrist fights against them and wins, but his fury grows because of their uprisings.

He aims his fury at Israel and, when the sixth angel sounds his trumpet, he takes advantage of the situation to begin the march to Armageddon.

With the sixth trumpet/vial, the Euphrates River (in modern day Iraq) dries up, freeing four fallen angels who had been bound in the river. These

47

angels are commanders of 200 million demon horsemen who have breastplates of fire and brimstone. The heads of their horses are like the heads of lions, out of which comes fire, smoke, and brimstone.

The horsemen spend 13 months on earth, killing one-third of the earth's already dwindling population with the fire, smoke, and brimstone from their own mouths. They also torture people with their tails, which are described to be like serpent's heads (Revelation 9:19).

The mayhem caused by the seals and the trumpet/vial judgments pleases the devil. He thinks the demons God has set free increase his power against God. And with the Euphrates River dried up, a pathway is opened for the kings of the east to ride into Israel for the Final Battle, so Satan takes the opportunities that are opening up to him and sends out three unclean spirits to gather the kings of the world together for war against God (Revelation 16:12-16).

Ezekiel explained in his prophecies of the end times that the three spirits of Revelation 16:13 are sent out to gather the kings of (1) Meshech and Tubal; (2) Persia, Ethiopia, and Libya; and (3) Gomer and Togarmah (Ezekiel 38,39).

1) Today, Ethiopia and Libya are the same nations that they were during Ezekiel's time, but much smaller. Persia reached from modern day

India to Greece, encompassing what is now Iran and part of Afghanistan. During the end times these countries will grow in might, power, and size. This is not only possible but is highly probable because each country sits on reserves of oil, natural gas, and other minerals.

Ethiopia, for example, has left its natural resources untapped for decades. Ethiopia, which is now poor and reliant on other countries for financial and military aid, will become a major world power because the world turns to her for resources.

2) Meshech and Tubal are not the names of countries, but are sons of Japheth, Noah's son. God showed Ezekiel that the other nations would constantly change over the centuries, so He called the areas by the names of Noah's descendants who settled there. Japheth became the father of the Caucasian people (Genesis 10:2,5), and historical records show that Meshech and Tubal (Russian and Slavic peoples) settled near the Black and Caspian seas, which are currently bounded by Turkey, Romania, Bulgaria, the Ukraine, Iran, and former Soviet southern republics such as Georgia, Azerbaijan, and Kazakhstan.

3) Gomer, the son of Japheth, and Togarmah, Japheth's grandson, settled further west and north in Europe. Their descendants now live in Austria, Italy, France, Sweden, Germany, the former

Yugoslavia, etc.

The kings of these three federations are part of the Antichrist's confederate nations and have the biggest armed forces. Because they doubt the Antichrist, he must lure them into action by using the supernatural powers of the three unclean spirits. Although the Antichrist's other allied nations are part of this army that converges on Israel at Armageddon, Ezekiel's three countries are the major forces.

National boundaries and forms of government change so fast that I would be wrong within a year if I gave the current names of the countries that are a part of the Antichrist's confederacy. For instance, what was Yugoslavia became Bosnia-Herzegovina, Serbia, Croatia, Slovenia, Macedonia, and others in 1992; West and East Germany were reunited as one nation in 1990; and in 1989, the Soviet Union broke off into more than a dozen independent states.

What I can say is the Antichrist's confederacy of 10 nations (whether they are 10 nations we can recognize today or 10 new nations) will come out of the area surrounding the Mediterranean Sea, covering Europe, the Middle East, and northern Africa.

Daniel's prophecies give us this information. Nebuchadnezzar's dream of an image with a golden head, silver arms and chest, brass stomach and thighs, iron legs, and feet of iron and clay (Daniel 2), was the same as Daniel's dream of four beasts, a lion, bear, leopard, and iron image that had 10 horns (Daniel 7).

The gold head/lion represented Babylon, the silver arms and chest/bear represented the Medo-Persians, the brass stomach and thighs/leopard represented Greece, the iron legs/iron image represented Rome, and the iron and clay toes/10 horns represented the Antichrist's kingdom.

These visions correspond with the beast of Revelation 13, which is described as having seven heads and 10 horns that are each crowned; and of Revelation 17, which is described as having seven heads and 10 horns. This beast is the Antichrist.

John explains the beast's seven heads: *". . . are seven kings: five are fallen, one is, and the other is not yet come; . . . "* (Revelation 17:10). The seven kingdoms are those that afflicted the Jews when they were a nation. So, the first five kings are Egypt, Assyria, Babylon, the Medo-Persians, and Greece. The one that "is" in John's day was Rome. And the one that is yet to come and will *". . . continue a short space"* (Revelation 17:10) is the Antichrist.

The 10 horns are the 10 countries which ally with the Antichrist. They come out of the boundaries of these seven kingdoms.

America

Will America be a part of the Antichrist's confederacy and end-time army? No. The Antichrist does not conquer the whole world, only the part of the world that was once the Roman Empire. America was not part of any of the seven world empires that afflicted Israel.

As the Antichrist becomes more aggressive against Israel, America, the countries that were once part of the British Empire, and some other nations revolt against the Antichrist. Ezekiel calls these countries, *"Sheba, and Dedan, and the merchants of Tarshish, with all the young lions thereof, . . . "* (Ezekiel 38:13). Again, Ezekiel uses the descendants of Noah to describe the nations.

Dedan and Sheba are both descendants of Ham. Dedan's people settled on the northwest shores of the Persian Gulf (Genesis 10:7), including northern Saudi Arabia and Kuwait. Sheba and his family settled on the southwest shores of the Persian Gulf, including southern Saudi Arabia, Oman, and the United Arab Emirates. Today the peoples of Sheba and Dedan are mostly Arabs and are mortal enemies of Israel, but when the Antichrist creates a peace treaty between the Arabs and Israel, they keep their word and protect Israel.

Tarshish was Noah's great-grandson who settled in the western Mediterranean Sea (II Chronicles 9:21;

Psalms 72:10) near the Rock of Gibraltar in Spain. The merchants of Tarshish were famous for their ships (Isaiah 2:16; Jonah 1:3; 4:2) and their home was considered the furthest point in the world. Because Tarshish was as far away as one could possibly go (which is shown by Jonah's attempt to flee there when he was running away from God), it represented a distant but unknown land which, in the last days, has a world-wide influence. The "young lions" are offshoots of that country or commonwealth.

Although Tarshish was in what is now Spain and the Spanish Empire had many off-shoots, I believe God is talking about Great Britain and her former colonies because these countries, including the United States, have greater worldwide influence than the former Spanish colonies. Even if the prophecy did refer to Spain, many parts of the United States were originally part of the former Spanish Empire and would therefore be part of the armies that come **against** the Antichrist.

Jesus Claims the Earth

While the Antichrist is luring the world's armies to Armageddon for the final showdown, the scene in heaven is triumphant. In Revelation 10:1-4 we see Jesus as He plants one foot on the earth and the other on the sea. This is not His physical return to the earth, instead it is the figurative move He makes in order to restore the world to its rightful owners—mankind.

When the seventh and final seal is opened, Jesus fulfills the law of inheritance and proves He is the rightful heir to the world. By setting His feet on the earth, He legally claims the right to kick the trespasser, the devil, off His property (Psalms 24:1).

In another figurative move, Jesus gives the title deed to the earth to John and instructs him to eat it. This symbolizes mankind's legal inheritance to the earth. By eating it and finding it to be bitter in his stomach, John shows that the possession of the world is sweet, but the events that lead up to this moment cause great sorrow to the human race (Ephesians 1:11-14; Revelation 10:10).

Death of the Two Witnesses

The Antichrist watches as his empire crumbles, and in his fury he attacks those who have attacked him—the two witnesses. He kills them in Jerusalem and leaves their bodies lying on the street for 3½ days for the world to see (Revelation 11:7-10).

As people watch these events unfold on television, they rejoice at the death of the two witnesses, but then are amazed as they watch them come back to life and ascend into heaven (Revelation 11:11,12). As the two witnesses are being raptured, an earthquake in Jerusalem kills 7,000 of its inhabitants (Revelation 11:13). The stage is finally set for Armageddon.

Chapter Four
In the Valley of the Shadow of Death

The fury of the Antichrist is kindled by the resurrection and ascension of the two witnesses. They made a fool of him, and, in retribution, he decides to take his campaign against God and His people to the ultimate level. He declares war on Israel.

The Antichrist gathers his confederate armies in Armageddon (Revelation 16:16). Joel 2:2 says this army of the devil is like a "... *great people and a strong; there hath not been ever the like, neither shall be any more after it, ...*" So many soldiers are in this invading force that the sun is blocked by the dust they kick up.

Joel compares this multitude to the huge locust swarms of his day. Thousands upon thousands of locusts would come over the plains and mountains and block out the light of the sun. Their approach could be heard for miles. People knew that when the locusts came, so did destruction, and they knew that they could do nothing to stop their coming.

They're Coming!

Likewise, the people see and hear the coming of the Antichrist's army as they head east out of Armageddon and south down the Jordan River Valley. When they arrive at Jericho, they turn west towards Jerusalem.

In distress, the people sound the alarm. They blow the ram's horn, called a shofar, which is what the Israelites blew before battles. The horn makes low, guttural music, calling the people to arm themselves and prepare to fight.

As they prepare for this Battle of Armageddon, the Israelites must arm themselves ingenuously. During the last 3½ years, they have faced natural disasters, demonic attacks, and persecution from the Antichrist. Only a handful of guns, grenades, and other weapons remain after all the destruction and confiscations.

I believe they make weapons out of wood and other available materials, creating spears, bows and arrows, and "Molotov cocktails" (bombs made out of bottles and flammable liquids such as alcohol).

They can hear the Antichrist's army as it marches through Israel (Isaiah 10:28-34). The roar of the soldiers' marching, their machines, and their destructions echo through the air like thunder. The explosions they set off behind them ignite the sky like lightning.

Joel 2:3 says, *"A fire devoureth before them; and*

behind them a flame burneth: . . . ." So intent are they on destruction that the armies of the Antichrist set off bombs, including chemical, biological, and other deadly weapons, to turn the land of Israel into a "desolate wilderness." Their bombs sound and look like *" . . . the noise of a flame of fire . . . "* (Joel 2:5). They set Israel on fire.

The March of Death

Remember, this army is like none other. Nuclear weapons are the prime choice for destruction. There is no thought of conquering the country or protecting anyone's life or property. The intent of the devil and his army is to annihilate Israel and God's people. Generals do not weep when their battalions fall due to explosions and radiation; they push on and keep their eyes on the prize of Jerusalem's destruction.

Although it would be easier for the Antichrist to destroy Israel by simply launching a nuclear weapon into the country, I believe he will not be able to do this. The massive destruction to the earth by the seven seals destroy most, if not all, of the military's advanced technology, including missile launchers, radar systems, and more. Armies (not just the people in Jerusalem) have to use whatever is handy, including farm implements, to fight with (Joel 3:10).

Even though the technology is no longer available to launch the missiles, the nuclear warheads are still intact because they have been protected in subterranean silos. The Antichrist has the machinery of destruction available, but he is forced to bring it to his target on foot.

The Antichrist's army is extremely agile (Joel 2:4) and uses horses and maybe even tanks and other armored vehicles to help them move with unity and precision through the valleys, mountains, and rough terrain of Israel. They don't break their ranks and are extremely precise (Joel 2:7). Satan's force is the most disciplined fighting machine the world has ever witnessed.

Joel 2:8 says, *"Neither shall one thrust another . . . ."* In Hebrew, this phrase says the soldiers do not "press the other," meaning they are extremely disciplined and trained. This is no hodge-podge attack; it is well-coordinated and organized. Every man marches in unison with the other. No one seeks attention or praise. They have a common goal and present a united front against God.

Another phrase in Joel 2:8 gives us insight into the army: *" . . . and when they fall upon the sword, they shall not be wounded."* The English translation here is wrong because the Hebrew actually says: *"When they break through the defenses, they do not break ranks."* I have no doubt in my mind that Satan gives his men incredible strength and agility, but he is not able to keep them from dying. He has too many soldiers to care about the lives of a few thousand men, so there is no need to protect them. This army, however, is so coordinated that they march forward as one person—nothing can stop them.

All along the way they are raping and pillaging before they destroy the villages and towns of Israel as part of the devil's plan to torture God's people.

The Attack

When the armies finally arrive in Jerusalem, they attack ruthlessly. The soldiers rush on the city and climb the walls, beginning the work of war: *"They shall run to and fro in the city; . . . they shall climb up upon the houses; they shall enter in at the windows like a thief"* (Joel 2:9). They ransack, rob, plunder, and strip bare the houses, rape the women, and take half the people into captivity (Zechariah 14:2).

The people in Jerusalem react with fear and horror and are in tremendous pain and anguish (Joel 2:6). Their faces *"gather blackness,"* which means they turn pale with fright as they realize the enormity of the army that has come to attack them.

Multitudes in the Valley of Decision

Then, when the soldiers are through looting and attacking, they leave the city and gather in the Valley of Jehoshaphat, which is part of the Kidron

Valley on the east side of the city between the Temple and the Mount of Olives. The Antichrist has prepared his nuclear weapon and the troops are assembling to leave the area so he can detonate the device.

Although the army thinks it is following the commands of their demon-general, it is actually following God's plan, who calls the army into *"the valley of Jehoshaphat"* in order to deal with and judge them (Joel 3:12). (The name, *Jehoshaphat*, means "Jehovah judges.")

When they get into the valley, everything becomes pitch black. God darkens the sun and moon and stops the stars' shining for 24 hours (Joel 3:15; Zechariah 14:6). It is as if time stands still. Their machinery doesn't work and they can't see to march or walk. Each and every soldier is forced to remain where he stands.

God calls the Valley of Jehoshaphat the "valley of decision" in Joel 3:14 because, during the 24 hours of inactivity and calm, God gives the nations of the world one final opportunity to repent of their sins—it is His final "wake-up call" to their spirits (Joel 3:12).

Throughout time, God has always shown people His character. He has revealed His glory through nature, the stars, the miracles of life, His Word, and His people. During the Tribulation, He sent angels to witness, had 144,000 people tell His story, gave the two witnesses the power to work miracles, and sent supernatural judgments. Even after all of that, God still gives the people who reject Him and rebel against His love and authority one more opportunity to change their minds. He even gives them the peace and quiet they need to think clearly about their situation because God does not not send His judgment on anyone until He has first shown His mercy.

During this same 24 hours, God deals with the people who remain in Jerusalem. Many are still alive, but they are bleeding, beaten, and frightened. When the darkness descends, I believe they wonder what kind of trouble has befallen them again, but then they hear the Lord speak to them, saying " . . . *Turn ye even to me with all your heart, and with fasting, and with weeping, and with mourning: And rend your heart, and not your garments, and turn unto the LORD your God: for he is gracious and merciful, slow to anger, and of great kindness, and repenteth him of the evil"* (Joel 2:12,13).

Repent!

I think this call to repentance is very beautiful and so typical of God. For centuries the Jews have rejected God in so many ways. At the very beginning of their nation, they worshipped golden calves, brazen idols, and hateful gods of heathen nations even though they had received the most powerful demonstrations of God's love and mercy. They still doubted and refused His presence.

They later rejected their true Messiah but accepted a heinous lie of the devil, the Antichrist, as their "savior." In choosing Satan's lies of physical peace and prosperity, they showed God that His promise of inner peace and soul prosperity wasn't good enough.

Through it all, however, God's anger against them was slow to boil. His every step, judgment, and sign through the ages was given to show them the truth of Who He is and Who they are in Him. He never gave up on them, returning time and again to purchase them from the pit of their sins.

His final attempt to get the Jews' attention is very loving. He speaks to them in the darkness and tells them, "Today is the day of your salvation." Their situation couldn't be worse; but in the midst of it all, God talks to them, wooing them into the safety of His arms (Joel 2:12).

He wants them to give Him their hearts and to show repentance through fasting, weeping, and praying. They can't truly repent and accept the Lord's sacrifice without some sort of outward evidence of their changed natures. Even if they don't show their emotions, God wants them to break their hearts in repentance. People who only make the outward show of tearing their garments aren't saved; God chooses those who break their hearts in true repentance to be His own (Joel 2:15-17).

Sometimes people "go through the motions" of repenting but don't mean it. An example is the story of Cain and Abel. Both offered sacrifices for their sins, but one gave with a broken heart (Abel) and the other gave, not out of real emotion, but as an act of responsibility (Cain). For this reason God accepted Abel's sacrifice of repentance, but rejected Cain's.

You can see the difference in the meanings of the word *repent*. Jesus told the people to *" . . . Repent: for the kingdom of heaven is at hand"* (Matthew 4:17). In this verse, *repent* is the Greek word, *metanoeo*, which means "to think differently." He was calling people to change their lives by changing their mind or attitude. This is true repentance.

However, when Judas *" . . . repented himself . . . "* (Matthew 27:3) after he betrayed Christ, he had a change of emotion. The word *repent* here is the Greek *metamellomai*, which means "to care afterwards." Judas was remorseful, but he didn't change his heart or his life. This is repentance in name only.

When the Jews repent at the Battle of Armageddon, God promises to be gracious and merciful to them. He forgives them of their sins and protects them. God offers His people the solution to this and every problem they have. In this time of distress, God helps them because they turn to Him and ask for help.

When the Jews accept God's call and ask for His help, they blow the trumpet, sanctify a fast, and call a solemn assembly. The priests weep to the Lord in intercession for the people. They accept Jesus' sacrifice and beg Him to return quickly (Joel 2:15-17).

The Marriage Supper

While all this is happening on earth, a great event is unfolding in heaven—the Marriage Supper of the Lamb. The saints and angels gather to witness this event.

The Bride of Christ, who is all the believers who awaited His first coming, who accepted Him after His death and Resurrection, and those who asked Him into their hearts during the Tribulation, are arrayed in the linen of righteousness, washed clean and white by the blood of the Lamb.

Christ enters the chapel on a white horse, His eyes are as flame of fire and crowns on His head; His clothes are dipped in blood.

The ceremony is a call to war and when it is finished, His saints mount white horses to follow Him (Revelation 19:7-14).

Christ's Return

God responds to the trumpet call of His people

in Jerusalem and He orders the seventh trumpet to be blown in heaven. With a *" . . . roar out of Zion, . . . "* (Joel 3:16) Jesus returns with His army, His Bride.

The army of the Antichrist doesn't turn to Jesus while in the valley of decision. Their choice is judged by God, and they are sentenced to death and eternal damnation. Jesus' war cry (the Word of God) becomes the Sword of the Lord and slays the Antichrist's army. Their blood flows in a river 200 miles long and four feet deep (Revelation 14:20). I believe this river of blood will flow in the Jordan River Valley, which is 200 miles long from the Sea of Galilee to the area south of the Dead Sea.

This battle is the harvest in which Jesus separates the wheat from the chaff (Matthew 3:12). The chaff blows away to the place of unquenchable fire, but the wheat remains and becomes the bread of life that blesses the earth during the Millennium.

Nature responds to Christ's return with lightning, thunder, 60-pound hail, and an earthquake that shakes the world (Jeremiah 10:10; Matthew 24:29-31; Luke 21:25-27; Revelation 11:15-19; 16:17-21). Islands and mountains move and entire cities are destroyed, including Egypt and Edom (Joel 3:19).

Babylon receives the full brunt of God's wrath as He destroys it with fire coming from heaven and an explosion in the earth. This is the same way Sodom and Gomorrah were destroyed

(Genesis 19:24,28; Isaiah 13:19; Jeremiah 51:47-49).

Babylon falls in a day. No one survives and no one will ever live in the city again (Isaiah 13:20,21; Revelation 18:6-8). This leads me to believe that the bomb intended for Jerusalem instead levels Babylon.

This destruction of Babylon is also a judgment of cults, false religions, and idolatry, all of which were pictured as the whore of Revelation 17. With the return of Christ, the nations realize the whore's deception and destroys her once and for all (Revelation 17:16,17).

Jerusalem

Jerusalem changes dramatically at the Second Coming. When Jesus' feet touch the Mount of Olives, the mountain rips in two all the way from the Mediterranean to the Dead Sea, which is 1,200 feet below sea level. The waters of the Mediterranean rush into the Dead Sea, carrying with it many of the soldiers whose bodies are scattered over the countryside. This new river flows from Jerusalem (Zechariah 14:4,8), which has been divided into three parts (Revelation 16:19).

Flesh-eating birds, which have been invited to the Supper of the Great God by an angel, feast on the bodies of the soldiers (Revelation 19:17,18). The smell of decaying flesh saturates the air (Joel 2:20).

One of the best outcomes of the Battle of

Armageddon is that the Antichrist and False Prophet are thrown into the Lake of Fire to be persecuted forever, Satan is chained in the bottomless pit for 1,000 years, and his demons are expelled from earth (Isaiah 24:21,22; Matthew 13:41-43; 25:41; Revelation 19:20,21; 20:1-3).

Christ takes possession of the earth and walks in victory through the eastern gate of His capital city, Jerusalem. His 1,000-year reign of the world has begun.

Chapter Five
The Day After

... *It is done* (Revelation 16:17).

When the smoke clears and the rumblings of the earth are silenced, the redeemed in Jerusalem look out of their walled city to see the countryside and mountains of Israel covered with the bodies of soldiers and their horses—hundreds of thousands of them—while vultures circle and land on the bodies for this great feast (Ezekiel 39:4,5,17-20).

All the people of Israel and travelers who pass through the land spend the next seven months burying the dead. The valley where they bury the Antichrist's army is just east of the Mediterranean. They rename it the Valley of Hamon-gog, which means "the company of Gog," who is the Antichrist (Ezekiel 39:11-16).

People go through the land, gathering their own weapons and those of the Antichrist's fallen army to use as fuel for their stoves and fireplaces. They use the spears, guns, and ammunition instead of wood, allowing the earth to recover and replenish itself after the seven years of destruction in the Tribulation (Ezekiel 39:9,10).

Men and women can no longer look to the works of their hands or the beauty of their world to bring them contentment or joy. They are no longer all-powerful or in control. Because of the state of the world, they are completely reliant upon God.

The plagues, earthquakes, hail, and fire destroyed man's churches, temples, mosques, and altars. His buildings, paintings, sculptures, and other creations are obliterated. The places man used to go to experience nature's beauty are gone. His earth is smoking, boiling, and in ruins.

Under Christ's supervision and with the saints' help, people of the earth begin the reconstruction of their homes. They cleanse the earth of the dead, plant their fields, and clothe their bodies.

The Restoration

Many people have incorrectly taught that the Millennium is a perfect time on this earth when humans receive glorified bodies and renewed minds, and nature is redeemed from its curse. This is wrong because the Millennium is a time of *perfecting* this world and its inhabitants, not of living in perfection. (The only people who live in *glorified* bodies are the saints who were raptured or resurrected before or during the Tribulation.)

The Word says that, during the Millennium, bodies need to be buried, things stink, people need to find ways to keep warm, and employment is necessary (Ezekiel 39:11,14).

The laws of nature remain somewhat unchanged because, while the world carries some old curses, new blessings begin to take shape.

Living waters spring from the house of the Lord—the Temple—and flow southward out of Jerusalem until the river breaks into two branches, one that travels to the Mediterranean Sea and the other to the Dead Sea (Ezekiel 47:1; Joel 3:18; Zechariah 14:4,8).

The river of "living" waters heals the Dead Sea, allowing a great multitude of fish to thrive in waters that were once so thick with minerals and salt that nothing could live there (Ezekiel 47:8,10). For the first time in history, the Dead Sea is a "living" sea.

Everywhere this river flows, a healing takes place. The river brings life to the desert and fresh water to a thirsty people and earth (Isaiah 35:1,2; Ezekiel 47:9). The entire physical nature of Israel is transformed into a land of abundance and growth.

Things change slowly in the Millennium but eventually the curse that is on the earth lessens so that deserts blossom and fields yield incredible harvests (Isaiah 35:1,2; Joel 2:22; 3:18; Amos 9:13-15).

The heavens change as the moon becomes as bright as the sun and the sun's light increases sevenfold. However, even the stars reveal that nature is not the source of life; it is God alone Who is the Source because the light of the Lord and the glory of God will give us the light by which we see, work, and play (Isaiah 30:26; 60:19-20).

Disease and destruction become memories as all creatures, men and animals, learn to live together in peace and harmony. The lion lies down with the lamb and men *"... beat their swords into plowshares, and their spears into pruninghooks: ... "* (Isaiah 2:4; 11:6-8). War as we now know it never again darkens this planet.

Mankind

Human nature, however, doesn't fall in line with God's plan as easily as nature does. People still rebel against Christ, but His salvation is available to redeem those who continue to sin.

Many people who survive the Tribulation and Battle of Armageddon are non-believers. However, when Satan is bound (Revelation 20:3), he is no longer able to deceive. People's eyes are opened to receive a unique and startling revelation of God's character and glory (Isaiah 11:9; Ezekiel 43:2). I believe at this time most people change their hearts and give their lives to Jesus (Zechariah 8:23).

Some people continue to deny Christ and live in sin. Everyone living during the Millennium is blessed because the devil is bound, but they still have to make the choice to follow God and obey His Word.

In today's world, we often say, "The devil made me do it." Although he deceives and tries to destroy us, Satan **doesn't make us** do anything. *We make the choice* to rebel against God and reject His Word. Likewise, the people in the Millennium make the choice to sin, but without the luxury of saying, "The devil made me do it," because he will not be around to lead anyone into temptation.

Christians in the Millennium receive the tremendous blessing of salvation in its fullest form. Christ gives them true inner peace, love, righteousness, and complete physical healing (Isaiah 9:7; 11:5; 32:1-3; 33:24; 35:5,6; Ezekiel 36:25,26).

Long life is restored to people. Isaiah 65:20 says a child "dies," or becomes an adult, at the age of 100. Lifespans probably reach to 900 or 1,000 years. However, death is not eradicated at this time.

The population of the earth diminished drastically in the Tribulation and Battle of Armageddon, but during the Millennium it increases rapidly. This baby boom proves that people still fall in love, get married, and raise families during the Millennium in the way God planned when He created man (Genesis 1:28).

The Reign of Christ

The first thing Jesus does when He sets up His earthly kingdom is assemble the people together. His angels gather His people from earth and heaven so He can sanctify this incredible congregation of flesh and blood humans and glorified saints as they enter into the Millennium with Him.

The word, *millennium*, isn't a fancy theological term, it simply is a Latin word that means "a thousand years" and refers to the length of time that Christ and His saints rule and reign over the earth.

The saints (who arrived with Christ on white horses and received glorified bodies and minds when they were raptured or resurrected), reign with Jesus as kings and priests and help Him guide the nations, bringing a perfect form of government to the world (Revelation 20:4).

God heads this world government through Christ (Daniel 7:13,14), Who reigns over the world from the Temple in Jerusalem (Isaiah 2:2-4; Zechariah 6:12,13). God's purpose through this government is to restore a righteous and eternal government on earth as He originally planned (Isaiah 9:6-7; 11:1-9; 42:1-5; Daniel 2:44,45; Luke 1:32,33; Revelation 11:15; 20:4-6; 22:4,5).

King David, in his glorified body, rules over all Israel under Christ (Ezekiel 37:24-28); and the 12 apostles rule over one tribe each (Matthew 19:28). The Jews who were redeemed during the Battle of Armageddon become the head of all nations under the Messiah (Deuteronomy 15:6).

During the Millennium, God restores the years that the locust ate, giving the Jews all the land and blessings He had promised to Abraham, Isaac, Jacob, and David (Genesis 13:14; 15:17; Isaiah 60:21; Joel 2:25).

At the beginning of the Millennium, Israel receives all the land east of the Mediterranean Sea and Nile River and west of the Euphrates River. Generally, the new Israel covers the land that is now Egypt, Sudan, Ethiopia, Somalia, Saudi Arabia, Oman, the United Arab Emirates, Kuwait, Iraq, Syria, Turkey, Jordan, and Israel.

The gentile nations receive land according to God's plan (Deuteronomy 32:8; Acts 17:26), and all nations are required to send representatives to Jerusalem once a year to acknowledge Christ at the Feast of Tabernacles (Zechariah 14:16-19; Isaiah 2:1-4). Those countries that are not represented at the feast will be cursed with a plague and drought.

The Levitical priesthood is reestablished and serves in the Millennial Temple (Acts 15:13-18), preparing all the former offerings, feasts, and rituals of the Temple as a form of worship and to show men Christ's redeeming work through the pictures of the rituals (Ezekiel 43:19-27; Isaiah 66:19-24). It is similar to us taking communion.

The Jews evangelize the nations in a one-world religion that blesses all nations (Isaiah 2:2-4). The blessings of Christ's perfect government are the peace (Isaiah 2:4), justice (Matthew 5:1-7) and prosperity that fill the earth (Isaiah 29:17; Jeremiah 31:27,28).

The Rain of the Holy Spirit

Be glad then, ye children of Zion, and rejoice in the LORD your God: for he hath given you the former rain moderately, and he will cause to come down for you the rain, the former rain, and the latter rain in the first month (Joel 2:23).

Something which I consider extremely exciting is when the Millennium begins, the Holy Spirit is poured out on all flesh with tremendous power (Joel 2:28,29).

Joel refers to this outpouring of the Holy Spirit as the the former and latter rains. He uses this description because Israel's economy and society were primarily based on agriculture, and the former and latter rains had to do with harvest times.

The former rain was the moderate spring rain that came right at planting time to give the seeds moisture to germinate and grow. The latter rains came in the fall in large amounts to make the vegetables and fruit multiply and grow large. Together, these combinations of rain made a bountiful harvest that blessed people throughout the year.

The spiritual meaning of the passage has to do with the glory of the Lord in the Old and New Testaments. The former rain is God's Spirit poured out in the Old Testament; and the latter rain is His glory in the New Testament. You and I are living in the latter rain, which began on the day of Pentecost. This "rain" is poured out upon us so we can reap a bountiful harvest of souls.

At the beginning of the Millennium, something unique and wonderful happens because the latter and former rains come together and pour out upon all people, showering everyone with the glory of the Lord as He was, is, and will be.

The saints of the Old and New Testaments enter the Millennial reign of the Lord together. They will experience the glory that was revealed to Abraham, shone on Moses' face, guided and protected the Israelites by the pillar of fire and the cloud, and filled the wilderness Tabernacle and the Temple. And they will feel the power that was manifested on the day of Pentecost and has been pouring out for nearly 2,000 years. This is very exciting to me! I love the way the Holy Spirit moves on people today; it's hard to imagine how much better it can get. The presence of the Lord will truly be incredible during the Millennium.

Satan Unleashed

At the end of the thousand years, Satan is unleashed and allowed to roam the earth, gathering the sinners and rebels who remain. Satan's fury has only grown during the Millennium, and he sets out to finish what he started at the Battle of Armageddon.

The army reaches Jerusalem, but before anything can happen, fire comes down from heaven and devours the soldiers. God then throws Satan into the Lake of Fire, where he spends eternity in pain and torment (Revelation 20:7-10).

Judgment Day

With Satan and the people who denied Christ cast off the earth, God begins His final judgment of mankind. All the people who had denied Christ are resurrected from the dead in order to stand before God's Great White Throne.

God looks in the Lamb's Book of Life to find the name of each person who stands before His throne. This Book of Life contains only the names of Christ's followers. Those who are not found in the book are judged for the things they had done in life, based upon that which is written in the Book of Works, and then are thrown into the Lake of Fire (Revelation 20:5,11-15).

Finally, death and hell are cast into the Lake

of Fire and never darken the face of the earth again (Revelation 20:14).

The saints do not participate in the Great White Throne Judgment because they have already received eternal life. Only the wicked, unsaved dead take part in the judgment (Revelation 20:6).

We do appear before *". . . the judgment seat of Christ; that every one may receive the things done in his body, according to that he hath done . . . "* (II Corinthians 5:10). However, at the Judgment Seat of Christ, God does not recompense His children for their iniquities; we will only be recompensed for our "good" deeds so that we will receive rewards.

All Things New

For, behold, I create new heavens and a new earth: and the former shall not be remembered, nor come into mind. But be ye glad and rejoice for ever in that which I create: . . . the voice of weeping shall be no more heard in her, nor the voice of crying (Isaiah 65:17,19).

Now that the devil, his angels and followers, and all the bodies of the wicked have been removed from the earth and seas, the curse and wages of sin are finally lifted from man and earth.

God dwells with men on earth, where there are no more tears, death, sorrow, curse, crying, pain, or night. Sin and death are gone. The whole plan of redemption is now complete (Revelation 21:4, 22:3,5).

The new heaven and earth are not the result of an unrecorded catastrophe that occurs after the Great White Throne Judgment. They are the result of the process of restoration and regeneration that started with the Tribulation and was completed by Christ during the Millennium.

It is not possible for Christ to fail. So, to say that God destroys the world and creates a new one, even after Christ redeemed it, is wrong. The term *"pass away"* doesn't suggest destruction; it is a redemption expression that means former things are passed away.

Besides, why would trees applaud and mountains and hills break into song unless they had not once known the weight of the curse of sin and death and then felt that incredible burden lift? This new world is one of joy and godly substance, not a new creation. It is a world where there are no more thorns or thistles, no locusts, plagues, blight, mildew, or weeds (Isaiah 55:12,13).

The New Jerusalem

Revelation 21 and 22 describe the New Jerusalem, which comes down from God out of heaven, casting down the glory of God over the world and giving it light. The city has a great wall with 12 gates of pearl. It is made of gold, with walls of jasper, decorations of precious stones, and streets of gold.

The River of Life flows from the thrones of God and Christ, and the tree of life, which was once in the Garden of Eden, stands in the midst of the street on either side of the river. It yields its fruit every month and its leaves heal the nations.

Holy Jerusalem is the home of the bride, the saints whose names are written in the Lamb's Book of Life. The saints come to live here after the Millennium to fulfill the promise Jesus gave them when He said, *"In my Father's house are many mansions; . . . I go to prepare a place for you"* (John 14:2).

This city is the capital of the universe because God's throne is in it. Its citizens are the kings and priests who give the world the benefits of the water of life and the leaves of the tree of life.

From the creation of the world to its restoration, God has continued to show us that He loves us and wants us to accept His salvation. He doesn't want us to change, but to accept the love and redemption from Christ that will change us. We have learned that we are powerless to make ourselves sinless, perfect, and holy; only Christ in His redemptive work can accomplish this. What a wonderful message of hope, salvation, and redemption God has given us!

What About You?

The events described in this book are events that will happen in the future (I believe the not-too-distant future). Do you know where you will fit into God's plan for this earth? Will you be part of the overcoming Church that is raptured before the Tribulation? Or are you a Christian in name only? I urge you to search your heart and see if you have truly asked Christ to be the Lord and Master of your life.

This message of Armageddon is meant to inform and inspire you, to help you understand Biblical prophecy, and to prepare you and your loved ones for events that will happen soon. I also want this book to encourage you as a Christian.

When you understand the events of the end times, you understand how perfect God's plan and purpose are for this world and His people. The wicked rule and reign now, but that is coming to an end because God's purpose for the Tribulation, Armageddon, and the Millennium is redemption and regeneration for the world and for mankind.

These events may seem too hard to imagine, but they are only extreme versions of what is going on in a person's life before Christ. Because of original sin, your life without Christ is a perfect battleground for Satan and it is in the same condition as the world is at the present time— overrun and controlled by wickedness.

Have you experienced tribulations in your life? Have you gone through famine, battles, physical suffering, or natural disasters as the result of your own, your family, or this world's sin? These tribulations are difficult to live through, but the Holy Spirit is always there to "woo" you into God's arms.

When Christ is not Lord of your life, the forces of evil will converge on your soul (mind, will, and emotions) with the ultimate goal being the conquest and destruction of your spirit.

Through it all, God calls you to repent. When you do, Christ comes into your heart and breaks it open. As Christ rules and reigns over your life from the Temple in your heart, a river of life begins to flow out of your spirit, giving nourishment and new life to your body and soul.

The enemy is defeated in your life, but it still takes a while for things to be restored, healed, and regenerated in your soul and body. You are governed by a perfect spirit which repairs what sin has broken—your body and soul.

It's important to remember that God gives you time to change. If He gives this planet 1,000 years to become perfect, then you know that He gives you, His blessed child whom He bought with a tremendous price, time to change and become whole. Don't blame yourself for mistakes, just return to Christ and ask for help and guidance.

In the end, you will become a new person whose life shines the light of God on others, whose spirit bears fruit in remarkable ways.

Are you experiencing tribulations in your life? Have things become so desperate that you feel the devil is doing battle in your heart? Do you want to be saved from this attack and be redeemed for a life of eternal fellowship with a Savior Who is gentle, loving, and perfect?

Then, pray with me today, *"Lord, I repent of the evil in my life, of the years I rebelled against You, and the times I rejected You. I accept Christ's sacrifice and ask Him to come into my heart to rule and reign over my life. I ask You to redeem me, restore me, and prepare me for eternity. I pray this in Jesus' blessed name, Amen."*

Appendix I

HARMONY OF REVELATION
Chapters 4–11 and 12–16

HEAVEN	EVENT	EARTH
4:1–3	Rapture	12:1–5
4:4–11	Saints in Heaven	
5:1–7	The Seven-Sealed Book	
5:8–14	Saints Sing the Redemption Song in Heaven	
	Satan Attempts to Prevent the Resurrection	12:3, 4
	War with Satan and His Angels	12:7, 8
	Satan Cast Down to Earth	12:9–12
	Satan Persecutes the Church Left Behind	12:13–17
	The Universal Power of the Beast	13:1–8
	The Satanic Trinity	13:11–18
6:1–8	The Four Horsemen — Gospel Preached by Agents from Heaven Amid Judgments and Plagues	14:6–20
6:9–11	Tribulation Saints Waiting Their Resurrection	
6:12–17	Earthquakes and Falling Stars Hinder Satan	12:15, 16
7:1–8	144,000 Saved Israelites Remain on Earth	14:1–5
7:9–17	All Tribulation Saints Raised	
8:1–5	Preparation for Seven Last Plagues	15:1–8
8:7	1st Trumpet Vial — The Earth	16:1, 2
8:8, 9	2nd Trumpet Vial — The Sea	16:3
8:10, 11	3rd Trumpet Vial — The Rivers	16:4–7
8:12, 13	4th Trumpet Vial — The Sun	16:8, 9
9:1–12	5th Trumpet Vial — The Seat of the Beast	16:10, 11
9:13–21	6th Trumpet Vial — The River Euphrates	16:12
10:1–11	Christ Takes Legal Possession of the Earth	
	Satan Counters by Marshalling His Forces	16:13–16
11:1–13	The Two Witnesses and Their Message	16:15
11:15–19	7th Trumpet Vial — The Return of Christ	16:17–21

Reprinted by permission from ALL THINGS NEW by Arthur Bloomfield; published and copyright 1971, Bethany House Publishers, Minneapolis, Minnesota 55438.

Appendix II

THE STRUCTURE OF REVELATION

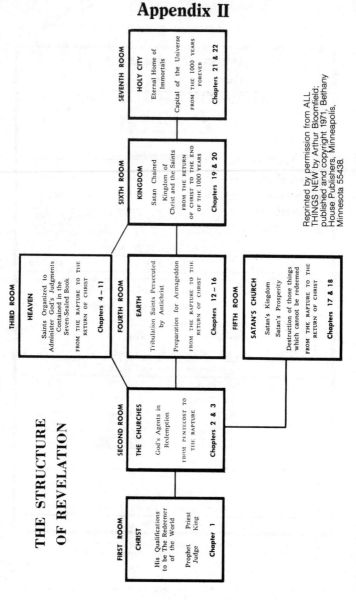

FIRST ROOM

CHRIST

His Qualifications to be The Redeemer of the World

Prophet   Priest
Judge   King

Chapter 1

SECOND ROOM

THE CHURCHES

God's Agents in Redemption

FROM PENTECOST TO THE RAPTURE

Chapters 2 & 3

THIRD ROOM

HEAVEN

Saints Organized to Administer God's Judgments Contained in the Seven-Sealed Book

FROM THE RAPTURE TO THE RETURN OF CHRIST

Chapters 4 – 11

FOURTH ROOM

EARTH

Tribulation Saints Persecuted by Antichrist

Preparation for Armageddon

FROM THE RAPTURE TO THE RETURN OF CHRIST

Chapters 12 – 16

FIFTH ROOM

SATAN'S CHURCH

Satan's Kingdom
Satan's Prosperity

Destruction of those things which cannot be redeemed

FROM THE RAPTURE TO THE RETURN OF CHRIST

Chapters 17 & 18

SIXTH ROOM

KINGDOM

Satan Chained
Kingdom of Christ and the Saints

FROM THE RETURN OF CHRIST TO THE END OF THE 1000 YEARS

Chapters 19 & 20

SEVENTH ROOM

HOLY CITY

Eternal Home of Immortals

Capital of the Universe

FROM THE 1000 YEARS FOREVER

Chapters 21 & 22

Reprinted by permission from ALL THINGS NEW by Arthur Bloomfield; published and copyright 1971, Bethany House Publishers, Minneapolis, Minnesota 55438.

Receive Jesus Christ as Lord and Savior of Your Life.

The Bible says, *"That if thou shalt confess with thy mouth the Lord Jesus, and shalt believe in thine heart that God hath raised him from the dead, thou shalt be saved. For with the heart man believeth unto righteousness; and with the mouth confession is made unto salvation"* (Romans 10:9,10).

To receive Jesus Christ as Lord and Savior of your life, sincerely pray this prayer from your heart:

Dear Jesus,

I believe that You died for me and that You rose again on the third day. I confess to You that I am a sinner and that I need Your love and forgiveness. Come into my life, forgive my sins, and give me eternal life. I confess You now as my Lord. Thank You for my salvation!

Signed _____

Date _____

Write to us.
We will send you information to help you with your new life in Christ.

Marilyn Hickey Ministries • P.O. Box 17340
Denver, CO 80217 • (303) 770-0400

Can You Read the Signs?

Call (303) 796-1333 to order!

End-time prophecy is being fulfilled on the pages of today's newspapers! Are we approaching Armageddon? Would you recognize the Antichrist? Let Marilyn lead you through the age-old Scriptures that reveal the prophetic significance of tomorrow morning's news. This tape set is a message of warning and of hope that you'll want for yourself and your loved ones! 3-tape set/#322 **$15.00** (U.S. dollars)

Offers good in U.S. and Canada only. Prices listed are in U.S. dollars; if using Canadian funds, please calculate the current exchange rate. To order, write Marilyn Hickey Ministries • P.O. Box 17340 • Denver, CO 80217.

Unlock God's Prophetic Timetable

Call (303) 796-1333 to order.

Here's your opportunity to get a grasp of Bible prophecy, better understand Christ and the Antichrist, and hear about the end-time revival of the Jews! You'll also discover the ten pictures of Jesus in this action-packed book of the Bible and learn details of the approaching Great Tribulation and the Second Coming of Jesus. 4 videos/V14H **$50.00** (U.S. dollars)

Offers good in U.S. and Canada only. Prices listed are in U.S. dollars; if using Canadian funds, please calculate the current exchange rate. To order, write Marilyn Hickey Ministries • P.O. Box 17340 • Denver, CO 80217.

LIMITED EDITION

ZECHARIAH
Last Days Prophecies

■As seen on the "Today With Marilyn" Television Program ■

By Marilyn Hickey

FOR YOUR VCR!

MARILYN
HICKEY
BIBLE
COLLEGE

Explore your options and increase your knowledge of the Word at this unique college of higher learning for men and women of faith. The Marilyn Hickey Bible College offers **on-campus and correspondence courses** that give you the opportunity to learn from Marilyn Hickey and other great Bible scholars, who can help prepare you to be an effective minister of the gospel. Classes are available for both full- and part-time students.

For more information, complete the coupon below and send to

Marilyn Hickey Bible College
P.O. Box 17340
Denver, CO 80217
(303) 770-0400

Name Mr.
       Mrs.
       Miss _____   Please print.

Address _____

City _____ State _____ Zip _____

Phone (H) _____ (W) _____

Prayer Requests

Let us join our faith with yours
for your prayer needs. Fill out below
and send to
Marilyn Hickey Ministries
P.O. Box 17340
Denver, CO 80217

Prayer Request _____

_____

_____

_____

_____

_____

Mr. & Mrs.
Mr.
Miss
Name Mrs. _____

Address _____

City _____

State _____ Zip _____

Phone (H) (   ) _____

(W) (   ) _____

☐ If you want prayer immediately, call our
Prayer Center at (303) 796-1333,
Monday – Friday, 4:00 am – 9:30 pm (MT).

For Your Information
Free Monthly Magazine

☐ Please send me your free monthly magazine OUTPOURING (including daily devotionals, timely articles, and ministry updates)!

Tapes and Books

☐ Please send me Marilyn's latest product catalog.

Please print.

Mr. & Mrs.
Miss
Mrs.
Name Mr. _____

Address _____

City _____

State _____ Zip_____

Phone (H) ( ) _____

(W) ( ) _____

Mail to
Marilyn Hickey Ministries
P.O. Box 17340
Denver, CO 80217
(303) 770-0400

BOOKS BY MARILYN HICKEY

A Cry for Miracles ($5.95)
Acts of the Holy Spirit ($7.95)
Angels All Around ($7.95)
Armageddon ($3.95)
Ask Marilyn ($8.95)
Be Healed ($8.95)
The Bible Can Change You ($12.95)
The Book of Revelation Comic Book ($3.00)
Break the Generation Curse ($7.95)
Daily Devotional ($5.95)
Dear Marilyn ($5.95)
Divorce Is Not the Answer ($4.95)
Especially for Today's Woman ($14.95)
Freedom From Bondages ($4.95)
Gift Wrapped Fruit ($2.00)
God's Covenant for Your Family ($5.95)
God's Rx for a Hurting Heart ($3.50)
How To Be a Mature Christian ($5.95)
Know Your Ministry ($3.50)
Maximize Your Day . . . God's Way ($7.95)
Release the Power of the Blood Covenant ($3.95)
The Names of God ($7.95)
The No. 1 Key to Success— Meditation ($3.50)
Satan-Proof Your Home ($7.95)
Save the Family Promise Book ($14.95)
Signs in the Heavens ($5.95)
What Every Person Wants to Know About Prayer ($3.95)
When Only a Miracle Will Do ($3.95)
Your Miracle Source ($3.50)
Your Personality Workout ($5.95)
Your Total Health Handbook— Body • Soul • Spirit ($9.95)

MINI-BOOKS: 75¢ each
by Marilyn Hickey

Beat Tension
Bold Men Win
Bulldog Faith
Change Your Life
Children Who Hit the Mark
Conquering Setbacks
Experience Long Life
Fasting and Prayer
God's Benefit: Healing
God's Seven Keys to Make You Rich
Hold On to Your Dream
How To Become More Than a Conqueror
How To Win Friends
I Can Be Born Again and Spirit Filled
I Can Dare To Be an Achiever
Keys to Healing Rejection
The Power of Forgiveness
The Power of the Blood
Receiving Resurrection Power
Renew Your Mind
Solving Life's Problems
Speak the Word
Standing in the Gap
The Story of Esther
Tithes • Offerings • Alms • God's Plan for Blessing You
Winning Over Weight
Women of the Word